Acclaim for *Let Her Lead*

"I am so gratified to know my friend, Brady Boyd, is standing with those in the larger church community who see women in ministry leadership as timelessly intended by God and thus wholly consistent with the Holy Scriptures—both Old and New Testament. I urge leaders and other workers in today's church to read, be nourished, and join in seeing the whole Body of Christ activated for ministry."

—Jack W. Hayford, Chancellor, The King's University–Dallas/Los Angeles

"I've walked the halls of Brady's offices hearing his female staff members rave about how he lets them lead. I've also walked the halls of corporate America, wishing for more men like Brady who would let women lead. This small book is big on wisdom for the church and the marketplace."

—Lynette Lewis, Speaker, Business Consultant, Author of *Climbing the Ladder in Stilettos*

"*Let Her Lead* is a long-overdue book that deals with an issue that has haunted the church for centuries. It's time for the church to get it right as it relates to a woman's role in marriage, the church and society. As this book heals wounds in the hearts of women, it will bring understanding to the minds of men."

—Jimmy Evans, Founder and co-host, Marriage Today; Senior Elder, Trinity Fellowship

Let Her Lead

Creating a Better Future for Women in the Church

Brady Boyd

Let Her Lead: Creating a Better Future for Women in the Church

Copyright © 2013 by Brady Boyd

Cover art copyright © 2013 by Bondfire Books, LLC.

See full line of eBook originals at www.bondfirebooks.com.

Published in association with the literary agency of Alive Communications, Inc., 7680 Goddard Street, Suite 200, Colorado Springs, Colorado 80920
Electronic edition published 2013 by Bondfire Books LLC, Colorado.
ISBN 9781535314107
eISBN 9781625393067

Table of Contents

Introduction

On a bright November morning nearly thirteen years ago, my wife, Pam, and I showed up at Northwest Hospital in Amarillo, Texas, ready to pick up our adopted daughter, Callie, who was to be born that day. After the hours-long whirlwind that surrounds every child coming into this world — the anticipating, the monitoring, the laboring, the delivering — finally a tiny, red-haired, blue-eyed girl was placed in our arms.

As Pam and I prepared to leave the hospital, Callie's birth mom looked at me and, with a slight upward nod toward my new daughter, said, "Brady, make sure she's always a daddy's girl."

Coming from her, I knew what that meant. She'd always had a good relationship with her father, and at the tender age of nineteen still treasured being a daddy's girl. She wanted the same care and acceptance for Callie that she herself enjoyed. *Let her be seen*, she was saying. *Let her be heard. Let her be valued and adored and loved well.*

Of course, she didn't need to issue a reminder. Little girls — and big ones too, for that matter — are always treated this way. Right?

Callie is twelve years old now, almost thirteen, making the ridiculously quick hop between girlhood and womanhood right before my eyes. Boys ease into puberty the way winter gives way to spring, as evidenced by my son, Abram, now fourteen. It's subtle. It's slow. It happens in fits and starts, flying under the radar most times. But girls? One day they're a mish-mash of giggles, pigtails and pink swim floaties, and the next day they're full-on woman, see them flourish, hear them roar.

This transition has got me thinking not only about the twelve-year-old "woman" who now resides in my abode — and at five-foot-seven, Callie's frame, at least, is precisely that — but also about the world she will inhabit once she enters adulthood for real. What kind of interests will she hope to pursue? What kind of friends will she choose to have? What kind of bosses will she wind up working for? What kind of people might she lead? What kind of faith community will surround her? What kind of man will she marry? (That last question leaves me blank. My daughter still wants nothing to do with the opposite sex, which is totally fine by me.)

But to my point: Given all the promise and potential awaiting Callie, how do I help prepare her for her future? And how do I prepare that future for her?

These are the central questions banging around my brain as I sit down to write this brief book. We're going to have a conversation about a topic — women in leadership — that is touchy for many people, especially church people, but I'm not trying to be provocative here. I'm not trying to pick a fight. I actually want to defuse this topic that has been infused with such vitriol along the way by simply revisiting a few themes that have been sidelining women far too long.

But I also want to begin by admitting that, as a

dad, I cringe at the thought that in ten or twenty or thirty years, my bright, capable daughter could have doors slammed in her face for the simple fact that she happens not to be male. If she is cut out to be a corporate CEO, then I hope she'll be hired. If she is cut out to be President of the United States—perhaps even the first female one, if Hillary doesn't get there first—then I hope she'll be elected. If she is cut out to be a professor or a lawyer or an engineer or a horse trainer, then I hope she'll be chosen there too.

And if she is cut out to lead within the church, then I hope she'll be *invited to lead.*

If I were to boil down my desires, dreams, assumptions, and plans for the type of world that will embrace my daughter, they'd fit into two simple manifestos: Let her be *her.* And let her be *heard.*

This isn't just my vision for the world ten or twenty years from now, when Callie is a bona fide adult. It is my vision today, here, in our present culture. There are 30- and 40- and 50-year-old women who want to engage in leadership now. What I want for Callie is the same thing I want for them: to be seen and heard, acknowledged and valued, loved well and led well... and learned from by both women and men.

We've been turning an important corner at New Life Church, in Colorado Springs, Colorado, where I've pastored for almost six years. For the first time in our church's nearly thirty-year history, women are excelling in senior-leadership roles. Licensed female pastors in our body are preaching the Word of God, teaching what Christ-followership means, baptizing new believers, counseling troubled souls, dedicating new babies to God's purposes, praying over those both near to and far from God, administering the sacrament of Communion, leading, serving, prophesying—in essence, doing *everything* female leaders did in Scripture. And they are doing these things incredibly well.

Now, depending on your upbringing, your predispositions, and your denominational bent, you are either heartened or horrified by this news. Trust me, regardless of which end of the spectrum happens to reflect your perspective, I understand your view. It occurs to me that if I were caught in the church of my youth even hinting at the idea of women preaching and teaching and leading, I'd be deemed a heretic and tossed out on my ear. Really. They would not so quietly shout "apostate!" and erase my name from the record books.

But if they (and also you?) simply would hear me out, before the tossing-out-on-my-ear, here is what I would say: "Some of what I believed thirty years ago, I discovered just wasn't true. And some of what I discounted, I learned was really real. What I didn't know, I now know. And what I knew for sure I now doubt."

Then, I'd let them toss me out on my ear. And oh, how quickly they would.

So, to the "what I believed thirty years ago that I

have since discovered just wasn't true": despite the rigorous language used during my youth to convince me otherwise, men need to get out of the way of women leaders so they can walk in the freedom that's been theirs all along. Female leadership in our homes, in the workplace, and in the church matters. It happens to matter a lot.

Maybe a brief story will help.

In his memoir, *The Pastor*, Eugene Peterson tells of his young mother — she was only twenty-three or twenty-four at the time — taking toddler Eugene with her every Sunday night to churches where she would preach the Word of God to miners and lumberjacks scattered in small, out-of-the-way settlements throughout the Rocky Mountain region, all year long, during hot summers and cold winters alike.

It was the Depression era in the United States, and Eugene's dad, determined to "put bread on the table and meat in the pot"[1] at the Peterson home, would spend those evenings working long hours to build his self-started butcher shop. Eugene writes, "I have no idea how this young woman with a child as her chaperone managed to gather a congregation of working men from those logging and mining camps to sing gospel songs, listen to gospel stories, and let themselves be prayed for on those Sunday nights in the thick of the Depression."[2]

The part of the story that Eugene left out of the book but will tell you in person is that a few years into his mom's mining-town ministry, a Pentecostal pastor from a nearby community—a male pastor—told Eugene's mother that as a woman, she had "no business" leading worship services. He commanded her to stop.

Tragically, she did.

Still, in the brief time that she followed God's leading, she led countless lumberjacks to the Lord even as she unwittingly rebelled against the norms for women in those days. In Eugene's words, "my mother, without knowing what she was doing, was developing an imagination in me for being a pastor." And aren't we glad she did.

We are glad, aren't we? Despite our theological differences—yours and mine, whatever they may be—I think we both would be grateful for every woman who has bucked propriety in order to raise a lover of God.

See, this is the sticky part of the subject regarding "women in leadership" in all its forms: we try to hang our hats on customary interpretation while avoiding what's happening in real life. We raise signs that shout, "Can't Teach! Can't Preach! Stay Silent! Sit Down!" but then read a story like Eugene's and go, "Wow. What a woman she was."

It's perplexing, to say the least. But despite the myriad questions—*why the genders? why the squabbles? why the how-much-should-women-do confusion?*—here are two things I know for sure: women are valuable to God and therefore must be valuable to lovers of God. And, secondly, when the history books are written, I want my name to appear on the side of ledger of those who sought to see women freed.

At this writing, one-third of the 56,000 students in seminaries accredited by the Association of Theological Schools are women, compared with one-eighth 10 years ago and almost none 20 years ago.[3] Three out of 10 seminarians today are women; follow the trajectory to its logical conclusion, and women will be the majority of seminary grads soon. And who knows what new realities that one actuality will usher in. Frankly, I'm open to what unfolds, as God swells wisdom, enlarges capacity, expands minds. In the meantime, I rest in the knowledge that the Grand Answerer to all of our questions is not up there wringing his hands.

So, let's take a look at what God intended for women, back when Eve burst onto creation's scene. Let's look at some modern-day realities surrounding women and ask what God intends for them now. And let's see what answers we can find.

Chapter 1: Let Her Be Her

A woman's worth has been substantial all along. A quick read of the first chapter of Genesis reveals three helpful truths about humankind—women, as well as men—and while we may debate the timing, order, and priority of the creation scene, what's known for sure is that **divinity**, **unity**, and **diversity** were involved. Men and women were created in God's divine image; men and women walked in unity with God, and also with each other; and men and women were men and women. They were different one from another, per God's perfect plan.

Divinity

God's original posture toward humanity was not at all ambivalent: he created them—male and female alike—in his glorious image, and he purposed them—again, male and female alike—for three primary tasks. They were to reign over the animal kingdom; they were to fill the earth and subdue it; and they were to enjoy the creation around them, this paradise laid out by a loving and generous God.

The triple occurrence of "they" here is important. God did not create only man in his image; he created woman that way too. God did not task only man with dignified work; he tasked woman that way too. "They" ruled together, sharing authority and dominion equally. Which is kind of ironic, because before the curse of the fall made people power-hungry and petty and corrupt, nobody had any use for authority, dominion, and clout. "Both men and women were responsible to fulfill their ministries of service for God's glory," my friend Bill Hybels says, "in the manner God had gifted them and to the degree to which they had been apportioned faith."[4]

In other words, women were not created as afterthoughts, add-ons, or additives, like the kind I put in my truck's gas tank, to give me a little boost. No, they were an *integral part of the deal*, from the very beginning of time. God welcomed his first divine daughter in a pretty powerful way: he referred to her by the Hebrew term *ezer kenegdo*, which translates in English to "helpmeet" or "helpmate." As the NIV version of the famous verse has it: "The Lord God said, 'It is not good for the man to be alone. I will make a helper suitable for him" (Genesis 2:18).

But before your mind rushes to *Aha! I knew it! This guy wants all women to only serve men! Barefoot and pregnant and submissive and subdued. I knew this is what a man would suggest!*—let me note two key items.

First, let's keep in mind that if God intended woman's sole role to be nothing more than an obedient, subservient sidekick to her husband, then any woman existing in a state of singleness would be living outside of God's will. Obviously, this is not the case.

And second, of the twenty-one times the phrase *ezer kenegdo* is used throughout Scripture, sixteen of them are used to refer to God himself. For example:

> "Hear, Lord, and be merciful to me. Lord, be my *help.*" (Psalm 30:10)

> "We wait in hope for the Lord; he is our help and our shield." (Psalm 33:20)

> "House of Aaron, trust in the Lord — he is their *help* and shield." (Psalm 115:10)

> "Blessed are those whose *help* is the God of Jacob, whose hope is in the Lord their God." (Psalm 146:5)[5]

God uses the same name for Eve that he uses for himself, which means that unless God had a massive inferiority complex, he had something more in mind than woman as congenial add-on to man.

Rather than referring to Eve as a second-class citizen, he says, "Think of it this way: I am what Eve was meant to be for Adam. And I am the great I Am!" Listen, Eve was created to show up for her mate. She was meant to do more than submit. I love how one author puts it: "If Adam must think for, decide for, protect, and provide for the woman, she actually becomes a burden on him — not much help, when you think about it. The kind of help man needs demands

19

full deployment of her strengths, her gifts, and the best she has to offer. His life will change for the better because of what she contributes to his life."[6]

"Helpfulness," in the Genesis sense of the term, is about as far as you can get from the idea of woman as lesser-than, dumber-than doormat/assistant/slave. Women, according to God, are valuable. They matter deeply to him. And therefore deeply matter to us.

~ ~ ~

I'm from the south, which is often a wonderful thing and sometimes a perplexing one. Perhaps perplexing things happen up north; I know for sure they do down south. For example, in various southern states whose identities I'll keep to myself, I have seen firsthand this troubling dynamic: A mom and a dad have both a teenage daughter and a teenage son. Sometimes the boy is older; sometimes the girl. Both are—relatively speaking—responsible, reliable kids. Both get good grades, or both excel at sports. Both tend to run with "good kids." Both customarily show respect and kindness and love. But despite all these similarities and good qualities, the daughter is treated differently than the son. The daughter has a twelve-o'clock curfew; the son can stay out as late as he wants. The daughter is told no when she asks for a cell phone, but the son is handed a slick new iPhone, because the boys get the toys, right?

The daughter has to bum rides off friends every weekend; the son is freely given the keys to his parents' cars. The daughter is encouraged to find a "nice young man" to marry; the son is slipped college applications left and right. At social gatherings, the daughter is asked to "join the women" in the kitchen; the son is invited to play pool or watch sports. The daughter is kept on an ultra-short leash, while the son is left to explore the world.

As I say, maybe this kind of backward behavior is at work in places such as Montana and Michigan and Maine as well, in which case, *mea culpa* to my southern friends. To all people in all geographies: *Stop the madness. Please.*

We are saying something about the value of a woman when we diminish her experience of life on this earth, especially while simultaneously elevating the experience of men. And if you think this differentiation of young boys and young girls is harmless and has no bearing on future behavior, think again. In research compiled for her book *Lean In*, author Sheryl Sandberg found that in a clinical test, **"if you ask men and women questions on totally objective criteria, men inaccurately assess their performance slightly high, while women inaccurately assess their performance slightly low."**[7]

Women do not believe they are valuable. Which stands to reason, given we have told them this is so.

When by our assumptions and our actions we ask women to be seen but not heard, to be pretty but not powerful, to be courteous but not challenging, to be amiable but not ambitious, to be submissive but not smart…when we expect them to merely cook and clean and change diapers, to show up but not speak up, to wear doilies on their heads during church services and *whatever you do, keep your thoughts to yourself*, we are saying something weighty about their value, about the worth of their very lives. And what we're saying, in my view, just ain't that great.

But the inverse is also true. When we prioritize the divinity in people, we esteem them — men and women alike. We honor them — men and women alike. We raise up their God-given value — men and women alike. We practice mutual surrender, mutual submission — as men, and as women, alike. We buck the trends of our wayward culture, which demands that a woman's value equates to her chest size, her sex appeal, her charm. And it's happening younger and younger these days. If you've seen the reality show *Toddlers and Tiaras,* then you know exactly what I mean. When overzealous parents are trotting out three- and four-year-old girls in fishnets and full makeup and asking them to glance coyly over their shoulder so that the judges will boost their scores, we've got a problem on our hands. Here's what we're telling those future women: "If you want the world's attention, you'll have to be overtly sexual to get it. If you expect to compete in this 'man's world,' if you ever hope to be valued or heard, then swinging your hips and shimmying your shoulders is really your only choice."

When we minimize the worth of women, we minimize the worth of her Maker. This is never a wise thing to do. Jesus says, "I came for the sake of freedom." We're to be about freedom too—freedom from suppression, freedom from marginalization, freedom from bondage, freedom from anything that lessens the value of womankind.

We enslave women and girls not just when we trick them into lives of destitution and servitude or when we trade them across borders as sex slaves—and for more than 20 million, tragically, this is their current lot—but also when we leave them feeling trapped in a world that values them only for the size of their breasts. We begin to free them when we plant more helpful seed, and then water it until a useful harvest bursts forth: "You are the apple of your Father's eye!" we can affirm. "And your value is not lost on me. What you see is valid, and what you're experiencing is meaningful. The thoughts you think? The questions you keep? The dreams you're dreaming these days? Rest assured that all of this really matters. It matters to God, and it matters to me."

People who walk through life with confidence do so because they believe that their life has worth. If we want to help our girls confidently step into their God-given roles in this world, we must reinforce the fact that they indeed matter to us. A practical example, from the frontlines of my own home: For as long as I can remember, I've told my daughter Callie that she is free to one day marry anyone she wants as long as two things happen to be true: the guy has to love Jesus with all of his heart, and he has to treat Callie as well as or better than I do. Admittedly, I've set the bar high. I've chosen to love her with such fully formed, godly love that the half-baked "love" from some pimply faced sixteen-year-old boy is probably not going to appeal to her. It will be nothing more than an unsatisfying substitute, sort of like being served greasy fast food when you've been in a five-star restaurant all your life.

I put these stipulations on giving my daughter away as a bride because in doing so, I take one step toward redeeming divinity in her. I tell the world that she is valuable, that she is a reflection of goodness and of grace and of God.

Unity

Not only was divinity evident at creation, but unity was present and prized too. When God breathed into life the start of humankind, the earth's first authentic, life-giving community was formed. Adam couldn't experience community with animals; God knew he needed one that was "suitable" for him. Hence, woman. And when Adam's "bone of my bone, flesh of my flesh" suddenly came to life, I have to believe there was an audible gasp. This wasn't a matter of hierarchy; it was instead one of biology[8]: two people, one flesh, one God to lead their way. For the first time — and, as it turns out, the *only* time for a while —

perfect unity was having its way. Mutual submission, mutual love, mutual respect, mutual service — God's vision for humankind had finally become real.

Fast-forward to last week, in the halls of New Life Church. A woman in her early forties approaches me following a worship service and asks about my perspective on something. "It's my marriage," she says. "I feel like there's no hope for us." She explains the dynamic that has been unfolding in her home for the better part of fifteen years and then offers up a recent example. She and her husband were having trouble coming to agreement on a big decision regarding his job, the outcome of which potentially would affect where they lived, where they worshiped, and where their kids went to school. "When I told him my perspective," she says to me, "my husband said, 'I hear you, but I don't agree with you. And since I'm the boss, we're going to go with my plan.'"

This is not exactly the vision God had for our homes and our houses of worship, when he lovingly breathed into life humankind. In the Garden of Eden there were no power-grabs and no trump cards; there was no dissonance, no one-upmanship, no swagger. Who gave the orders? Who made the decisions? It's simple: God, alone, was in charge.

When we prize unity in our relationships — those comprising males and females alike — we evict the egotism that always takes us down. "One gender holding power over the other" writes John Ortberg, "was not God's plan laid out at the beginning of creation. It is clearly here part of the *curse*.... Why would we cheer part of the curse?"[9]

Ortberg rightly assesses the famous verse that encapsulates the consequences of the woman's grave sin: "He [God] told the Woman: 'I'll multiply your pains in childbirth; you'll give birth to your babies in pain. You'll want to please your husband, but he'll lord it over you'" (Genesis 3:16). You'll recall that two chapters earlier, childbearing was presented in grand and glowing terms: Be fruitful! Multiply! Fill the earth and subdue it! Now, though? Not so glowing, and certainly not so grand: Pain. Pain multiplied. Your babies will only get here through pain.

Same goes with marriage: In Genesis 2:18, 24, we find God reflecting on the man he had just created and determining that it's not good for him to be alone. What he needs is a helper comparable to him. Yes, woman. That ought to do. The plan, then, was this: the man will leave his mom and dad and become "one flesh" with his beautiful bride. Sweet, right?

But then comes sin. And with it, the sweetness falls prey to subjection. He says, "I'm the boss, so we'll just go with my plan." To which she thinks, "He's hell-bent on being the head of this home? Fine. But I'll be the *neck*."

Nice attitude, eh?

We get exasperated with the opposite sex, thinking, "Well, this is just how God made it to be. Look! It says it right there in Genesis: this is part of his plan, after the Fall." But what we fail to recognize is

26

that God's statement in Genesis 3:16 — "You'll want to please your husband, but he'll lord it over you" (NIV) — was not a prescription but a prediction. He essentially says, "Look out! This is where you'll both fall prey."

Our current relational quandary was cited as a consequence but never a command, which means we actually have a way out of this horrible mess. By our words and by our actions, we can start to reclaim God's original intent.

> Recently, Pam and I had a big decision to make, about how to contribute financially to a debt-relief initiative our church has undertaken. I guess I could have powered up, charted a unilateral course of action, and (politely) informed her of what "we'd" be doing. But why in the world would I do that? This is the woman who holds my heart in the palm of her hand, the one whose voice informs everything of significance I do. I've been married to Pam for more than two decades, and with precious few exceptions — mostly my fault, really — we have made key decisions together, unified, as one. I seek God. She seeks God. We come together and talk. We pray about what we're sensing. We choose as wisely as we know how. "A husband

and wife filled with the love of Christ together approach the real authority in their family and ask him — God — what he wants," writes Charles Trombley. Together, they fulfill his will."[10]

And, I would add, then I — alone — accept responsibility for the worthiness (or worthlessness) of the choice.

I see the theme raised up throughout Scripture of God blessing husbands who determine to include and look after their wives in this way.

> You husbands, be good husbands to your wives. Honor them, delight in them. As women they lack some of your advantage. But in the new life of God's grace, you're equals. Treat your wives, then, as equals so your prayers don't run aground. (1 Peter 3:7)

> The husband provides leadership to his wife the way Christ does to his church, not by domineering but by cherishing. So just as the church submits to Christ as he exercises such leadership, wives should likewise submit to their husbands. (Ephesians 5:23–24)

> Husbands, go all out in your love for

your wives, exactly as Christ did for the church — a love marked by giving, not getting. Christ's love makes the church whole. His words evoke her beauty. Everything he does and says is designed to bring the best out of her, dressing her in dazzling white silk, radiant with holiness. And that is how husbands ought to love their wives. They're really doing themselves a favor — since they're already "one" in marriage. (Ephesians 5:25–28)

Incidentally, I think there is a bleed-over effect here. When I get good at viewing Pam as equally valuable, equally insightful, equally capable of hearing from God, then I start to understand that *all* women are wired this way. I know there are evangelicals who can't get past Eve having been the first one to sin and like to draw all sorts of wild conclusions about modern woman's trustworthiness as a result, but Paul seems to go to great lengths here to remind us that they have equal access to grace. Don't we want that access on our side, instead of fighting it tooth and nail?

We husbands treat our wives with patience, tenderness, and understanding precisely because we are the "head" of the home. And last time I checked, our role was compared with that of Christ's posture toward the church, for whom he was willing to die.

Interestingly, I've never met a woman who was being led well and not enjoying it. There may be a few females out there who refuse to let anyone influence their life, but they are rare exceptions. When men joyously serve, women joyously surrender to that gift of service. Or, in the words of Trombley, "When husbands love the Jesus way, wives submit the Jesus way."[11] You'd think this was part of a grand plan, or something. You'd think Jesus laid it out as a big, bold strategy, for the sexes to actually get along.

Back to the financial-contribution example I mentioned: Pam prayed about a number that would require a real step of faith for us. I did the same and then approached her to compare notes. One rule would govern our ultimate decision: she or he with the highest number won.

Pam won. Evidently, she possesses a bit more faith than I do. Still, when we wrote that check, I did so with a grateful heart, not just for the God-given resources to contribute to knocking off the last of our church's debt, but also for a companion on the journey who loves to hear from God and who loves to obey what he asks her to do.

It's not lost on me that when the apostle Paul wrote the infamous "wives, submit to your husbands" passage in Ephesians 5, he would be sending that letter to a culture where the Temple of Diana (also called the Temple of Artemis) existed, a house of worship erected in honor of the goddess Diana, a many-breasted idol who was known as "the Mother without spouse" and "the Mother of all." In Ephesus, many women had simply moved past men. Deciding they could live better lives without them, they superseded men's authority and went on their merry way. And really, who could blame them? Women had been treated like property far too long. But still, Paul, said, "Wait, wait, wait. You have taken this whole thing way too far. You who are married, submit to your husbands. Do not run past them! In the same way the church defers to its head, Jesus Christ, you defer to the head of your home, your spouse."

I love that my spouse doesn't run past me. And it would never occur to me to run past her. The goal here, again, is unity — yes, within the context of marriage, but also as women and men relate with one another in the church, in the workplace, in the world. This is how we (all) must lead our homes, and this is how we (all) must lead our churches. Beginning with the crucifixion of Jesus Christ, there was, as the apostle Paul so eloquently said, "neither Jew nor Gentile, neither slave nor free, *nor ... male and female,* for you are all one in Christ Jesus" (Galatians 3:28, NIV, emphasis mine). It is unity that is the way of Christ. Anything less is neglect and, in its worst state, outright sin.

So yes, unity is to be prized by women, but also — and especially — by men. I believe men have an extra burden to bear when it comes to harmonious living and a establishing a unified front.

To make my point, let's review a little scene in the

book of Genesis, wherein we find a deceptive woman, and a man who is equally flawed. By way of review, a serpent tempts Eve, the woman, to eat the forbidden fruit. The woman passes the fruit to the man, who also takes a bite. Sinfulness bursts onto the scene, and soon thereafter, more than a few fig leaves are sewn, God goes looking for the once-happy couple, who now are hiding in the trees. God says to the man, "Adam? Adam? Where are you, Adam?" to which the man says:

> "I was afraid.
> Because I was naked.
> And so I hid."[12]

Alas, the jig is up.

God says, "Who told you you were naked? Did you eat from that tree I told you not to eat from?" (Genesis 3:11).

"Yes, Lord, I did," responds Adam. "Eve and I did this awful thing, I am horribly sorry, and I take full responsibility for whatever consequences may come our way."

Wait. Things didn't exactly go like that.

Here is what Adam really said: "The Woman you gave me as a companion, she gave me fruit from the tree, and, yes, I ate it" (Genesis 3:12).

By my count, it took Adam three tries to the get the bearer-of-responsibility thing right. First, he blames God: "The woman YOU gave me as a companion ..."

Second, he blames his wife: "SHE gave me fruit from the (forbidden) tree..."

And finally, third, after two failed attempts, he affixes the blame where it always had belonged: "Yes, I ate it."

I participated.

I chose.

I willingly, willfully ate.

I was the guy you left in charge, and it was on my watch that she and I failed.

To my male compadres, a reminder: You and I begin to restore the botched Genesis deal when we accept responsibility for what we—women and men together—do. I've often wondered if the consequences of that "original sin" would have been lessened had Adam simply showed up and been a man. Maybe there wouldn't have been outright pardon, but I guarantee God would have been pleased. It pleases God when we fight for unity. It pleases God when we refuse to move forward until unity emerges. It pleases God when we vehemently disagree with each other but insist on staying the course until some sort of consensus can be achieved.

It pleases God when as a group of believers we listen well, we pray well, we choose well the course of action we will take, and we (as men) then take responsibility for the consequences of that choice. It pleases him when we dismiss the win-loss mentality that has crept into society as a whole, the posture that says, "I'm here to compete with you. And I fully plan to win." In reality, we're here to complement each other. We're here to help each other to flourish and finish strong.

Diversity

Callie and I were having breakfast together one morning a few weeks ago, and somehow we happened upon this topic of gender differences. I waded partway through a dry, clinical definition but quickly realized I'd lost my audience. In an attempt to reclaim her interest, I said, "You know, it's the whole waffles/spaghetti thing. Like the book says, men are like waffles, and women are like spaghetti."

Clearly, she hadn't read the book.[13] She let out such an uncharacteristically loud laugh that I couldn't help but chuckle too. When she finally gathered herself, she said, "What in the world are you talking about?"

I considered finding another analogy, but thought better of it. There are some subjects a twelve-year-old just isn't going to get.

The point is this: women and men are different. There is diversity here. And it's divinely placed diversity, at that. Let me explain what I mean.

Even in the midst of an ever-increasing societal push for genderlessness, surely you and I both can acknowledge that between men and women, there are differences of note. *The Economist* once ran results from a scientific gender-based study revealing that men are better than women at mathematical problem solving, heavy-lifting, and physical aggression, for instance, while women are better than men at smiling, spelling, and indirect aggression, otherwise known around the Boyd house as being "in a funk."[14]

In my opinion, women are also vastly better at holding babies than we men. A quick example: A few weeks after I accepted the role of senior pastor at New Life, just before a worship service was to begin I bumped into Megan Anderson, wife of Jared Anderson, who was one of our worship pastors. As she approached me, I noticed that she had one of her children strapped to her front, a second child strapped to her back, and a third one walking alongside her holding her hand. She carried on a conversation with me, totally unfazed by all the humanity she was holding up, and as I walked away following our interaction, I thought, "See, a guy could never do that. He'd be sending up SOS flares in five minutes flat."

But the diversity God introduced involved more than capabilities, personality, and traits. The original him-and-her dynamic went far deeper than that. For starters, suddenly there was community. As I've said, without a companion "suitable" to Adam, there would have been no community for him. You don't have to be married to appreciate the nuances and richness that a social sphere including both men and women brings to your life. We need each other. Men need women, and women need men. We *both* need *both* of us.

And then there was procreation. If you and I

existed in an asexually reproducing reality, we'd all be exact replicas of our one parent. Would you really want that? Especially if you didn't get to choose which one? Plus, who wants to be spores and liverworts when we instead can be women and men? No, *far* more interesting and far more desirable is the system God set up. Two people — one male, one female — coming together to create from their joint DNA-pool offspring that would be simultaneously derived from both parents, while still remaining characteristically unique. The question isn't whether there are two genders, then. The question is *why*? What exactly did God have in mind here? Why two, and not four, or eight? How do the two he established — the female, the male — play into this long-standing leadership debate?

These are unanswerable questions, of course. Which is why the debate exists. There is much we just don't know about God's intention for our two-gendered life here on earth. But what we do know is that there are two, and that there have been two since the beginning of time.

A recent study caught my eye. The findings showed that

> female managers who behave consistently with gender stereotypes — prioritizing "work relationships" and expressing "concern for other people's perspectives" — were liked but considered to be ineffective. Those who were

seen as behaving in a more "male" fashion, on the other hand—who "act assertively, focus on work task, display ambition"—were seen as competent but roundly disliked.[15]

To broad-brush it, women leaders who behave like men are viewed as more credible leaders than women leaders who behave like women. Ridiculous, right? Women who are called to lead and who possess strong leadership gifting should not be forced to become masculine in order to fulfill a leadership role.

More on this in chapter 2, but for now, let's let her be her. She doesn't need to become like him. Let her—any her, every her—be all the her that God envisioned her to be.

~ ~ ~

I offer the reminders of divinity, unity, and diversity because much of what I see unfolding in local churches today stands in stark contrast to that original design. It seems a pervasive preoccupation with titles and power has replaced the push for harmony and respect, and I wonder if the unfortunate swap in our priorities leaves God shaking his head in disbelief. We can do better. We can lead better. We can set right what we've let go so wrong.

Chapter 2: Let Her Be Heard

It is my wife's fault that I am a fan of Adele. Pam got me hooked somehow, and now it's an addiction I'm compelled to indulge. If you've ever heard Adele, then you probably understand why. This woman can *sing*. And her lyrics can slay even a thick-skinned, non-emotional, chest-beating redneck like me.

Last week, I was on a flight home after a speaking engagement in Texas, piping Adele as loudly as my ear buds would go. Whatever song she was singing stopped my multitasking mid-task and made me take notice. I shook my head reflexively and thought, "I can't imagine what this world would be like without the voice of women." What if we had never heard Alicia Keys, Beyoncé, or Adele? What if we'd never read J. K. Rowling? What if we'd never seen the likes of Condoleezza Rice and Hillary Clinton rise to some of our nation's highest offices? I'm not endorsing 100 percent of everything they say, of course. I'm just endorsing the liberty they enjoyed in saying it.

Think about it. What if the world of social work had never known Jane Addams, the world of fashion known Coco Chanel, the world of cooking known Julia Child, the world of medicine known Marie Curie, the world of entertainment known Aretha Franklin, the world of cosmetics known Estée Lauder, the world of cultural anthropology known Margaret Mead, the world of domesticity known Martha Stewart, the world of justice known Sandra Day O'Connor, the world of compassion known Mother Teresa, the world of television known Oprah Winfrey, the world of literature known Virginia Woolf, the world of humanitarianism known Eleanor Roosevelt?

What if we'd never heard from Rosa Parks?

It's a staggering thought to me. What if these women had never been allowed to speak?

Closer to home for me, what if Callie's voice is never heard?

Maybe it's a crazy thought to you, but the truth is that countless women are living life muzzled, for fear of overstepping what Scripture says they "should" do.

Two passages of Scripture, in particular, are to blame — the infamous "silencing-of-women" sections. Here they are:

> Women should remain silent in the churches. They are not allowed to speak, but must be in submission, as the law says. If they want to inquire about something, they should ask their own husbands at home; for it is disgraceful for a woman to speak in the church. (1 Corinthians 14:34-35, NIV)

> A woman should learn in quietness and full submission. I do not permit a woman to teach or to assume authority over a man; she must be quiet. For

Adam was formed first, then Eve. And Adam was not the one deceived; it was the woman who was deceived and became a sinner. But women will be saved through childbearing—if they continue in faith, love and holiness with propriety. (1 Timothy 2:11-15, NIV)

It was the apostle Paul who wrote both of these, and depending on where people fall on that spectrum we talked about previously—whether they are heartened or horrified by my church's choice to elevate women in leadership—they either find these two entries to be necessary and universal, or else they find them outdated and largely irrelevant to what it means to follow Christ. They either believe Paul is here writing within his role as a divinely appointed messenger, or he's a misogynist, a woman-hater, a clod—or, at a minimum, an unreliable spokesperson for Christ who added a couple of conveniently self-serving insertions while writing the Scriptures God asked him to write.

What Does the *Whole* Bible Have to Say?

Here is a useful question to ask when we bump up against highly controversial passages in the Bible, regardless of the subject matter they address: Will we choose to read those words in light of Scripture, or will we read all of Scripture in light of those words? An example of what I mean: Nowhere in Scripture is there an official command to support the notion that it is shameful for women to lead or speak. You can search until your eyes pop out, and you will find no such law. So when we come to Paul's commands to the Corinthian church and to his protégé Timothy, they ought to give us a little pause. We ought to slow down and say, "Hey. Wait a second. These instructions don't seem to jibe with the rest of what the Bible has to say."

It's worth noting that in the days when Paul lived and wrote, women were not obligated to study the Scriptures as men were. As a result, women weren't knowledgeable about the Word of God. They'd never been given access to the synagogues—and yet now, in the first-century church, they had a place. They could *come*. They could *listen*. They could *worship*. They could *learn*. But the information they were hearing was so radical, so incredible, so life-changing, that they just had to know more...*right then*. And so, they'd interrupt. They'd ask questions. They'd dig around for clarity on what they'd just heard.

As you'd expect, this dynamic was a little distracting. Can you imagine speaking to a group of people and having someone in the audience raise her hand every fifteen seconds to ask a question? Wasn't there a more appropriate time and place for these newbies to sort out individual matters of faith? Paul thought so: he suggested that a better plan, at least for those who were married, was that they wait until after the gathering had dismissed and then voice their questions to their (presumably well-educated) spouse. (This interpretation isn't just my opinion; it is the opinion of biblical scholars who have devoted *decades* to the study of this matter.) The Holy Spirit spoke to Paul about the issues of Paul's day, just as he speaks to you and me here and now. Women did not previously have access to education, and once they were invited into environments of learning, they had to be taught how to exercise some restraint.

Here's how I frame Paul's argument, one that stands strong still today: leaders must first be learners. It's helpful if we happen to know what we're talking about before we open our mouths to speak.

A few verses before Paul told Timothy that women should be quiet and should not assume authority over a man, he charged Timothy to "oppose false teachers." And one of the ways Paul said Timothy would know he had found a fraud was that these teachers would speak passionately and eloquently about something *they knew nothing about.* "They want to be teachers of the law," he wrote of them, "but they do not know what they are talking about or what they so confidently affirm" (1 Timothy 1:7, NIV). This should be instructive for us. If moms and dads and teachers and other key influencers want to raise up a generation of female leaders, we can start by awakening young women's curiosity for the world around them, the material world and the spiritual world alike, instead of relegating them to diaper duty and kitchen patrol.

I mentioned earlier that in ancient times, women were not educated as men were. Women were treated as property, not as divine vessels capable of thinking deep thoughts and accomplishing great things. In Babylonian times and beyond, rabbis even prayed a three-part prayer that went something like this: "Thank you, God, for making me a Jew, and for not making me a slave or a woman."[16] Slaves were viewed as inferior people, and women were viewed as less than that. In such a culture, who would *want* to be a woman? Women were seen but rarely heard, they were taken for granted and never taught.

Thankfully, things have changed. I read just last week that in under-resourced places such as Pakistan and Afghanistan and sub-Saharan Africa, when you educate the young boys, they tend to leave the villages and go search for work in the cities. But when you educate young girls, they stay home, they become leaders in the community, and they pass on to others what they've learned. "If you really want to change a culture, to empower women, improve basic hygiene and health care, and fight high rates of infant mortality," the writers suggested, "the answer is to educate girls."[17]

Callie came home from school the other day, totally exasperated by the fact that her history teacher expects her to care about topics such as the original boundary lines of Mexico and the Louisiana Purchase and the ancient Aztec civilization. With slumped shoulders, rolled eyes, crossed arms, and a dramatic sigh, she informed me that she only wants to learn things that she will *actually use* in life. I took the bait.

"So, Callie, tell me what that category would include. What are you planning to do in life?"

She cocked her head to the side, challenging my challenge to her. "I don't know."

"Okay. So, you don't really know what you will do in life, which means you don't really know what kind of information will help you do that unknown thing well, right?"

"Right." It was more a mumble than a word.

"So, you're thinking you'd like to just settle for what you *think* may unfold and call it quits?"

"Yeah," she said, spirits rising. "Yeah! I'm good with that plan."

Suffice it to say, Callie may be good with that plan, but her father certainly is not. I don't want my daughter to lose her intellectual curiosity, and I told her so that day. I also bored her to tears with a story from my childhood, when I was just a little younger than Callie is now. So that you don't feel left out, I'll risk boring you with it too.

When I was in the fourth grade, my family lived in a tiny, insular town in East Texas. I wasn't super-smart in grade school, but I *was* super-curious. And as soon as I was taught to read, I became a voracious reader. Reading was my mind's way of escaping my small town and entering a big, brave world.

Over time, the books my teacher assigned to our class weren't challenging enough for me, and so she began sending me over to the high school library, located on the other side of the campus, during "reading hour," where I could select whichever books I liked. It was like I'd won the lottery every day, month after month after month. I still remember the feeling of holding James Fenimore Cooper's *The Last of the Mohicans* in my hands. I still remember the smell of those pages. They smelled like adventure to me.

I knew I'd never live during the 1700s and that I'd never witness the French and Indian War. But even at an early age, I also knew that understanding the past could inform my future, and that other people's stories were important to learn.

"The world is bigger than knowing how to buy groceries, how to mow a lawn, how to fill up a gas tank, and how to balance a checkbook!" I told Callie. "Don't you want to know *more*?"

My daughter simply shrugged.

And so it goes, during pre-teen years. Who knows, maybe in some regards I was apathetic at that age too. Still, I won't give this up without a fight. The world really is bigger than the practical to-do's of life, and it really is worth exploring. If we lose our intellectual curiosity, it's not too big a leap to envision losing our spiritual curiosity too. If we lose our sense of wonder over creation, do we lose our wonder for the Creator next?

I pray Callie never finds out. I pray that instead, she follows the lead of Mary, who is a marvelous model of a "learning woman." In the classic scene where she is featured, in Luke 10, Mary is found sitting at the feet of Jesus, shirking every other possible responsibility in favor of knowing God firsthand.

As the story goes, Jesus had stopped by Mary's sister's home for a visit, and as Jesus sat there in the living room, the workaholic sister, Martha, scurried about, making preparations for their guest, tending to chores, and griping (to Jesus!) that Mary was no help. Dishes stayed dirty, the house stayed dusty, and for all we know, lunch never got served. But none of this mattered to Mary; she was the type to seize *every* opportunity to learn — *especially* from the Master Teacher himself. Jesus would later say to Martha, "Mary has chosen what is better, and it will not be taken away from her" (v. 42).

That's what I'm after for Callie, that she would constantly choose the "better thing." Leaders are first learners, right? I'm committed to helping her learn.

What Did Jesus Do?

There's another question we can ask when we find biblical texts that stick in our craw: What did Jesus do? Since Jesus came to model life as it is meant to be lived, we can look at *his* life — his assumptions, his attitudes, his actions — and there find a guidebook for how we should live.

In the first century, women were not even allowed to testify, because their word could not be trusted. Or so the thinking went, anyway. But then, watch this: Following the greatest miracle of all time — the physical, bodily resurrection of the crucified Messiah, Jesus Christ — to whom did Jesus himself choose to appear, before he appeared to anyone else? *A woman.* Jesus' first words, post-resurrection, were spoken to Mary Magdalene: "Woman, why do you weep? Who are you looking for?" (John 20:15).

I think it was a calculated move. I think Jesus was saying, "Listen, I know the Law says you aren't a credible witness. I know this culture says that even if you see a crime take place right under your nose, there is nothing you can do about it, because your word simply doesn't count. But here is what I say: Your word is reliable to me. Your voice is valuable to me. And I choose *you* to deliver the good news of the most important event in history to the world at large. You are capable of receiving truth. You are capable of confessing truth. You are capable of telling the others that I am alive."[18]

During the entirety of his earthly ministry, Jesus treated women with equity and grace, always calling out of them their gifting, great growth, real strength. His deep concern for the oppression of widows, his praise for the widow's mite, his touching the unclean woman, his ministry to the woman at the well[19]—by his words and by his actions, Jesus refused to honor, follow, vindicate, or accept the traditional laws that kept women enslaved.[20] I often wonder, "How serious am I about living this way too?"

It's a very good question to ask.

One of my favorite passages in the Bible speaks of the period just after the Holy Spirit descended on believers for the first time and helps explain Jesus' treatment of women in his day. You remember the scene: The Spirit enables those gathered to begin speaking in "other tongues," and a crowd of onlookers found this to be so bizarre that they accused those believers of being drunk. At nine a.m. In the presence of the Lord.

The apostle Peter steps out to clear things up. "No, no," he says. "We're not drunk, as you suppose. It's just that we've all been filled with the presence of God, just as the prophet Joel long ago foretold."[21]

The prophecy he referred to is found in Joel 2:28-32 and goes like this:

> "In the last days," God says, "I will pour out my Spirit on all people. Your sons and daughters will prophesy, your young men will see visions, your old men will dream dreams. Even on my servants, both men and women, I will pour out my Spirit in those days, and they will prophesy. I will show wonders in the heavens above and signs on the earth below, blood and fire and billows of smoke. The sun will be turned to darkness and the moon to blood before the coming of the great and glorious day of the Lord. And everyone who calls on the name of the Lord will be saved." (NIV)

Lest you skim over the important stuff, let me draw your attention to the fact that not once or twice, but three times the prophet Joel mentions that not only men, but also women, will be actively involved in ushering in the kingdom, the new reality called the Age of Grace. The Spirit would be poured out on *all people*, he says. Sons *and daughters* will prophesy. Both men *and women* will receive the Spirit and speak truth. This was a game-changer, to be sure. Women, who in the Old Testament days of Joel would have been seen but not heard, acknowledged but not valued, and used for breeding but not beloved, at last were being freed. Freed to learn. Freed to serve. Freed to lead.

This was a big, big deal.

It's still a big deal today. Or it ought to be, anyway. As a dad, I view my first priority in parenting Callie as teaching her to hear and respond to the voice of God. Because of Joel's prophecy, as stated in Acts 2, Callie, who is a Christ follower, has full *access* to the Spirit of God. She has every capability her male counterparts have, to receive the Spirit, to receive truth, to speak truth out. My job as her dad is simply to help her learn to detect this divine "pouring out" and to let it start to guide her life. I take on this role in her life because when I study the Scriptures, this is precisely what I see Jesus doing in women's lives.

What is God Doing, Here and Now?

There is a third question we can pose when we're trying to sort out confounding texts; "What is God up to in our modern-day, here-and-now?"

You don't need to look far to find examples of women who, determined to help bring a little bit of heaven to earth, are stepping up to leadership's task. Breakthrough Urban Ministries in Chicago was founded by Arloa Sutter, a woman who got tired of seeing homeless men in her community spending yet another day hungry and isolated. She asked for access to an unused meeting room at her church and began serving hot coffee and bag lunches and a healthy dose of Christ-like kindness every day at noon. Today, Breakthrough serves more than one thousand adults each year by providing 24,000 nights of shelter and more than 70,000 meals.

Eighteen-year-old Katie Davis made headlines a couple of years ago when she defied her loving parents and brother by foregoing college, ditching her high school classmates who had declared her both class president and homecoming queen, breaking up with her boyfriend, and moving from Nashville to Uganda, where she knew exactly one person. Today, this young woman who is barely done with childhood herself is in the process of adopting thirteen Ugandan children and continues to run the ministry she founded, which feeds and educates hundreds of children there.

My friend Lynette Lewis went from a glamorous, senior-level position with Deloitte and Touche in New York City to founding Stop Child Trafficking Now, a group that targets the demand side of sex slavery by rescuing and rehabilitating trafficking victims.

These and scores of other examples reflect undeniable momentum being enjoyed by women today. They are sensing God's call on their lives. They are carving out opportunities where they can serve. And they are taking on the societal beasts of today.

Which raises an interesting question: Should they be serving in these ways? For those who insist on women remaining "silent in church" and women "never teaching men," we quickly bump up against a few ponderables, such as, Should Arloa Sutter be serving and discipling homeless *men*? Should Katie Davis be feeding and leading girls *and boys*? Should Lynette Lewis be educating women *and men* about the travesties of sex slavery today?

Versions of these questions have been around forever, it seems:

Can women sing in the church choir? (Singing isn't silence, after all.) Or, Can women lead a congregational prayer?

Can women serve as missionaries overseas?

Can women write books about God that may be read by men?

Can women deliver a prepared talk to a room full of women, if the person running sound for the conference happens to be male?

Can they teach Sunday school, even for classes including boys? Can they instruct their own *sons* in their own home, or does that somehow violate the spirit of the "don't teach men" command? That last one really strikes a chord in me, given that my mom was my primary spiritual influence for the entirety of my young life. My father didn't follow Jesus Christ until I was a grown man myself. To put it plainly, if Mom hadn't been allowed to teach me the Scriptures, I wouldn't have learned them at all.

All around the globe, these "ponderables" only persist. Right now, women make up 70 percent of the world's poor.[22] And in situations of dire poverty, everyone who has a pulse has to work, meaning two-thirds of families, don't have the luxury of a mom who puts aside gifting and passion and chooses to stay home with the kids instead. No, her full resourcefulness is critically needed just to keep those kids alive.

The situation is similar inside the church: if you've ever visited or read about one of thousands of tiny churches located in rural sub-Saharan Africa, then you know they are made up primarily of women and children. Men travel into city centers to find work, often meaning they are gone for weeks on end. If women should not hold leadership roles in the United States, then they should be banned the world over, right? And yet who in a right mind would suggest such a solution in communities where men just aren't around?

You see where I'm going with this. If we believe that God spoke to Moses in Moses's day and Joel in Joel's day and Paul in Paul's day, then we also believe he can speak to you and me now. And I believe one of the things God is saying is, "Let my daughters be heard!"

So, what might it look like for God's daughters

to be heard? This is the question I've been asking of myself, for oh, the past fifteen years. A couple of themes have emerged so far, themes that challenge and inspire me alike.

Let's Quit Sidelining Women to "Women's Work"

In Romans 12, the apostle Paul says, "If your gift is prophesying, then prophesy…if it is serving, then serve; if it is teaching, then teach; if it is to encourage, then encourage; if it is giving, then give…if it is to show mercy, then show mercy."[23]

Some will say that the earliest translations of this passage include the preamble, "I appeal to you, *brothers*," noting that of course what followed was relevant only to men. But didn't the Holy Spirit descend on both genders in Acts 2? Aren't all believers gifted to serve?

Yes, Paul was writing to a patriarchal culture. Yes, Paul was writing to the educated ones in his midst, which by definition were Christian "brothers," the men. But gifting applies to both halves of the church; all of us are expected to serve. He said as much in 1 Corinthians 11:5, when he gave instructions for when women pray and prophecy.

If you're meant to prophesy, then, *prophesy*.
If you're meant to serve, *serve*.
If you're meant to teach, *teach.*
If you're meant to encourage, *encourage.*
If you're meant to give, *give.*

54

If you're meant to show mercy, show *mercy.*

If you're meant to lead, then by all means, lead! Men and women alike. If you are a man called by God to lead, then *lead.* If you are a woman called by God to lead, then *lead.* Sort out your gift-mix, scour leadership opportunities that suit your capabilities and interests, and get busy serving the body of Christ. The fact is, we need you. We need all of us, bringing all of our gifts to bear on the mission Christ has asked us to complete.

Leading Inside the Home

Undeniably, some women are called to apply their gifts in the context of the home. If you are one of them, fantastic! Do it! Sound leadership is sorely needed in the home. For all the good the Feminist movement did for women, its fatal flaw was robbing mothers of the nobility of motherhood.[24] Yes, it provided women the right to vote, the right to political equality, entry into a workforce that had been staffed predominantly by men, movement toward equal pay, benefits such as paid maternity leave, and more, but I'm not sure any of these byproducts is worth losing the dignity of the role of *mom.*

The truth is that for some women, the strongest thing they can do, the godliest path they can pursue, the most compelling calling they can fulfill is to raise and teach their kids. My wife and I know plenty of women in this camp: they *can* teach, they *can* speak, and they *can* lead. They just don't prefer to do so outside of the context of the home.

And that is perfectly fine. Just ask Jesus.

Jesus proved that being born of a woman, nurtured by a woman, influenced by a woman, and protected by a woman are significant passages for humankind. When he descended from heaven and entered our human reality here on earth, he easily could have come walking out of the hills one day, fully man, fully alive. But he didn't choose this course of action. Instead, he came as a baby, born of woman's womb, the "sole portal of entry into the world."[25]

The sad truth of our culture today is that men are reduced to sperm donors and paychecks and women are reduced to birthers and suburban soccer moms. Neither represents either's higher calling. No wonder we're all at war with each other; we feel diminished and denigrated and as a result pass along that underlying bitterness and slow-burning rage to everyone we meet.

God says to man, "You have the ability to restore a sense of Eden, in my church and in your home." To woman, he says, "You have the ability to literally give life, to bring life into a world marked by death."

These are high, high callings, to be sure.

Listen, women are *good* at bringing forth life. Their muscular, skeletal, and reproductive systems are perfectly fitted for conception, for pregnancy, for the miracle known as new life.

Women are also good at guarding life. They have

ridiculously keen awareness of their children's physical and emotional needs. I saw a National Geographic documentary on lions that trailed a female lion and her three cubs as they fought for survival after their pride's male had been killed. She fought off crocodiles, elephants, hyenas, buffalo, and lions from other prides, all in the name of protecting her vulnerable young. One of the narrator's lines summed up well what I see in the lives of every mom I know: "Her cubs' survival is a hard taskmaster for her." Yes, motherhood is hard. But to be a mother is to live by a whatever-it-takes code, when it comes to fighting for her loved ones' lives.

Women are good at civilizing life as well. The famed woman of noble character described in Proverbs 31 bears this out: follow her around for a day or two, and what you'd find in her wake is goodness, orderliness, and strength. She plans well, she thinks well, she executes well, she serves well. She beautifies and she blesses; she civilizes and she creates. And she's no anomaly; *every* woman is wired in this way. "Written deeply into our [women's] being is a gratification for subduing or beautifying life," writes Sally Clarkson. Women are such great civilizers, and to look on the product of our [their] making will create more joy than you can imagine."[26]

I'm not playing into stereotypes here; it's just my humble observation that when they're operating at their peak, women bring with them wherever they go a sense of civility, a sense of order, a sense of peace.

I've always viewed Pam's and my roles within our home as interchangeable in many regards; but there is a delineation that always seems to hold true. While I may provide our kids a sense of *identity*, their *stability* comes from Pam. Women set the tone of our homes, and even the tone of our world. This is no accident, in my view. Grafted into women's divine design is the desire to bring forth, to protect, to add civility to this thing called life. My counsel to you, if you're called to marriage and motherhood and ministering to little ones' needs, is to step into that calling with your head held high and your heart opened wide in anticipation of all that God will do in and through you.

Leading Outside the Home

In the same way that some women are called to lead in their homes, some are called to lead outside the home as well. I think of Yvette Maher, a pastor at New Life who sits on the executive team. She excels in the context of our staff, and she excels in the context of her home, proving that just because a woman is sparkling in leadership doesn't mean she isn't fully surrendered to other, more domestic roles.

I've been interviewing a variety of women for the purposes of this book, and during one such conversation, I was asked this question: "Am I outshining my quiet, introverted, private husband by using my more 'public' spiritual gifts?"

The woman I was talking with is a fantastic communicator, a brilliant writer, and a keen strategist who loves to lead teams of people. Her husband, while intellectually her equal, is a computer salesman who does his best work in a one-on-one setting, behind the scenes.

Along the way, this woman has been told by male and female Christ followers alike that by using her gifts of speaking, teaching, writing, and leading, she is defying her husband's authority, she is somehow out of bounds.

I looked at her and said, "So, let me get this straight. According to the naysayers you've encountered, the Holy Spirit has given you powerful, spiritual gifts that you are supposed to subdue for the rest of your life."

She thought about it, then nodded. "Yeah. I guess that's essentially what they're asking me to do."

"Do you respect your husband?" I asked.

"Deeply," she said.

"So, when you use your public gifts, you're not motivated by a desire to outshine him, right?"

"Outshine him? I've never even thought of that."

I then asked, "Is there unity among the two of you? Meaning, is he bothered at all when you use your public gifts?"

"Absolutely not," she said. "He *wants* me to pursue this course and is constantly pushing me to serve and lead."

I told the woman to use her gifts.

I offer the same counsel to you. If God has gifted you to serve and lead, and you are passionate about serving and leading, and the people in your life to whom you are accountable see value in your service and leadership, then step up—*please*—and lead. Women walk around with their hands tied behind their backs because they are told—even by people inside the church—that they must not outshine their men. To which I say, "Huh?" I *love* to see women soaring, using their strength and talent in service to God.

We want to show the watching world the win-win nature of men and women complementing each other rather than competing with each other, remember? We want to manifest unity at every turn. I remember hearing Bill Hybels once say that one thing he learned from watching his wife, Lynne, come into her own as a leader of various causes was that women who are freed, challenged, and empowered to develop their gifts and pursue the passion planted in them by God do not become less loving wives or less devoted parents. On the contrary, they bring a greater level of joy and energy to every dimension of life.

This is what the naysayers are afraid of, right? That if you pursue your calling *outside* the home, you will neglect your calling inside it? Maybe what they're really afraid of is that if other women are freed up—to speak, to serve, to lead—they themselves will start itching for freedom too. And you know as well as I do that often, the road to freedom is paved by disillusionment, discomfort, and change. We fear change because it feels so different from that which we know to be true. It feels like shifting sand.

Certainly, I'm not suggesting that leadership outside the home is every woman's calling. I don't believe that it is. What I am suggesting is that if you are so called, then you need to know there is a world just waiting for you to respond. Be a Deborah, the prophet and judge who for a time served as Israel's Commander in Chief. Be a Phoebe, a strong church leader and teacher, a "deacon," even, who in modern terms could be considered the first commentator on the book of Romans. Be a Jael, the gentle and quiet warrior who happened to take down the opposing army's leader via a tent peg in the skull. Be a Huldah, an exceptional prophet who was summoned to be a truth-teller for the king of the land. Be an Esther, the brave queen who went against every known custom to implore her husband to save her people from death. Be a Priscilla, a business-minded church-planter and disciple-maker whom the apostle Paul referred to as a "co-worker in Jesus Christ." Be a Junia, one who was called "outstanding" among all the apostles. Be a Mary of Nazareth, who knew the Scriptures, who issued strong prophetic visions, who was utterly passionate about seeing justice served for the poor.

Be the female leader God has called you to be. Yes, leadership is an invitation, not a command. But if God is calling you to lead, then please—for the sake of us all—say yes.

Let's Invite Women to the Table *to Lead*

Women don't bear the entire burden as it relates to helping themselves lead well. Whenever I train up young men in my own church, I recognize that in all likelihood, I'm training the very people who will take leadership's reins from me. As you'd expect, I'm careful about what I instruct these men to do.

Related to helping women find their footing as leaders within the church, there are two pieces of advice I always give to men: Lay it down, and listen up.

Lay It Down. "Laying it down" means letting the spirit of service motivate everything you do. This is the closing exclamation point of the 1 Peter 5 leadership trifecta: "Watch over God's flock," Peter said, "not because you must, but because you are willing…; not pursuing dishonest gain, but eager to serve; *not lording it over those entrusted to you*, but being examples to the flock" (vv. 2-3, NIV, emphasis mine).

Frankly, this isn't easy to do.

It seems easier to issue commands. It seems easier to bark out orders. It seems easier to just boss people around because you can. Because you're the leader, you're the boss.

But God says: *Don't.*

Instead, he says, sacrifice. Surrender. Serve. Look beyond gender biases and stereotypes, and seek out the gifting God has planted there. Lean *in*, even though there are differences, instead of leaning *out*, because of outright fear.

Let me give you a practical example from a

non-ministry segment of life. I've noticed an interesting phenomenon, based on the countless men I counsel each week, many of whom have daughters at home: When those innocent, pigtailed angels become teenagers, dads aren't real sure what to do. Gone are the days when they can cuddle, wrestle, or sweet-talk their little girls, without stressing out over whether they're doing and saying the right thing. Teenage girls are women with children's brains—a challenging combination, to be sure. And since many men just can't sort out how to navigate this new (terrifying) landscape, they do the only thing that seems to make sense: they totally and completely withdraw at the exact time when their daughters need them to press in, to protect, to stay close. They need their father to walk with them, to fight for them instead of against them.

This is what grown women need from us too. They need men to walk with them and to fight for them, not because they are weak or needy, but because they are prized people deserving of our responsiveness, and our respect.

We lay down our discomfort and disillusionment, and we serve those in our midst.

Listen Up. And then, part two: men, you've got to listen up. For several years now, every Tuesday I have met with a group of ten to twelve people who help me prepare and critique my sermons. Some are theologians, some are arts leaders, some are teachers. All are brilliant. When we first began meeting, I said, "Listen, you're here because I value your input. I want you to feel total freedom to tell me if my talk stinks. Tell me what you're noticing, as you watch me preach. Tell me what I'm missing, as we hash through next week's message. Tell me the truth. That's why I have you here."

Do you know that it took almost a full year before anyone really shot straight with me? These leaders had never been asked to give input to the senior person in charge, and frankly, they were intimidated by the task. It took time to get them to speak up. It took time for them to believe that they really could be heard.

A couple of weeks ago—this is almost six years after I preached my first sermon at New Life, mind you—I was having lunch one with of the guys from that group. Partway through the meal, he said, "There is something I want to tell you. It has taken me almost a year to gain the courage to tell you, but I think I need to tell you…"

I said, "Go for it! Tell me. I'm all ears."

"Well," he said, "when you preach, you say, 'by the way' a lot. It's kind of a verbal tic of yours."

I thought about it for a second and quickly realized the guy was right. "I never noticed that before," I said, "but you are dead on, absolutely right. Thanks for telling me! I'll get that solved, by the way." (Ha, ha.)

And that was that. Candid chat; input gained; problem solved—bing, bang, boom.

Here is the part of the conversation that wasn't so easy to reconcile. "It took you a *full year* to tell me

64

this?" I couldn't help but asking. With a chuckle I said, "What, exactly, did you think would go down, upon your giving me this input?"

Sheepishly he said, "I didn't know."

"You didn't *know*?" I was incredulous. What kind of guy did he think I was?

It drove home a key point for me, which is that when certain systems have dictated restrictive behavior for a while, and then a new system seeks to set that behavior free, it can take some time for the long-awaited freedom to unfold.

As this relates to women, we must be hyper-intentional about issuing the invitation to participate, to speak up, to take her seat at the table, to *lead*.

~ ~ ~

As I've said, I am responsible for hiring the first female executive-team member New Life Church has ever known. A couple of days before the first meeting she would participate in, I went in her office, made sure I had her full attention, and said, "Yvette, you are part of this team because you are gifted to lead. You are not there as a token, as an add-on, as a political statement to anyone who may be watching. You deserve to be here, and your voice is valuable to the success of this team. During this and all future meetings, I expect you to lean in, speak up, and lead well."

Thankfully, Yvette has taken me seriously so far and in doing so is paving the way for countless other women to lead in our church.

Closer to home, I'm also committed to drawing out the wisdom and insights of my own daughter. Callie isn't a verbal person. I have buddies with tween daughters who constantly lament the fact that their ears are actually going to fall off their heads, given all the chatter they're subjected to day by day, but things aren't that way for me. Callie is deep waters. Pensive. Quiet. Chilled out.

One morning recently, I said to her, "Callie, I want to know what's going on in your heart. I want to hear your voice. I want you to tell me what you're feeling, what you're thinking about school and friends and boys. I want to know how life is affecting you these days..."

This was not news to my child; for as long as I can remember, I've been communicating these messages to her. And yet her contributions are few and far between. That morning, I think her exact, not-so-verbose response was, "Okay, Dad," and nothing more. But then the next night, during our dad/daughter date at a nice restaurant in town, totally out of the blue, my daughter burst forth with a three- or four-minute assessment of her life, her thoughts, her dreams. I hung on every word.

Callie's words are like manna to me; I value every single one. When she speaks, I listen. I listen very, very well. And while today she may not totally believe that her voice is valuable, I am committed to drawing her out until she is firmly convinced of this fact.

We listen. We listen *well*, knowing that the more we listen, the more likely it is that women will finally speak. What a great day that will be.

After years and years of research and contemplation regarding the issue of women in leadership, one realization I've come to is that regardless of which "side" I choose, I'm going to make somebody mad. But there is another realization I've come to, which is that if my stance on women in leadership winds up being a "mistake" I can't undo, I'd rather err on the side of freedom. I'd rather risk seeing women live free.

I much prefer the idea of Callie standing at my graveside one day, thinking, "My dad put so much wind in my sails that I thought he might actually shipwreck me," than for her to stand there thinking, "Just once, I wish I could have gotten out of the harbor. I wish I could have sailed on those crystal blue seas."

Afterword: To Ordain or Not to Ordain?

Inevitably, whenever I talk with folks about the topic of women in church leadership, questions surrounding ordination pop up. *Can women be ordained pastors? Can women be deacons and elders? Can women "really" lead?*

Depending on whether the people asking lean egalitarian or complementarian in their views, a reflexive "Yes!" or "No!" is what they're trolling for. Behind the "yes" is this rationale: *Of course women can be ordained! Aren't all human beings equal in the sight of God? Didn't the Holy Spirit descend on all believers—males and females—alike? Weren't women given the spiritual gifts too? Didn't Jesus come to earth and die and rise again in order to usher in a reality in which there is no Jew and no Gentile, no slave and no master, no woman and no man? Doesn't the Bible actually highlight females who led at the highest levels of the church?*

And behind the "no," this: *Of course women cannot be ordained! The apostle Paul said so: man is the head, not woman. If Jesus meant for there to be women church leaders, he would have appointed female apostles to signal his desire. Plus, look at the Old Testament: see any female priests there? And don't get me started on how it was a woman who first was deceived in Scripture—do you really want such a vulnerable person leading you? Oh, and you might want to take a look at the New Testament passages about the qualifications for elders, which are all couched in masculine terms.*

Given the apparently bulletproof evidence on both sides of the subject, it makes sense that brilliant biblical scholars have debated it for centuries. The fact is, whether you stand with the yes camp or make your home with the no's, the basis of your argument is correct. Human beings *are* all equal in the sight of God. And, equally true, the Bible states that the head of the woman is the man. The Holy Spirit *did* descend on all believers. And, equally true, the apostles Jesus happened to appoint, in spite of his ability to appoint whomever he chose, were male. And on and on the arguments go.

The point about qualifications for elders being couched in masculine terms is one that's always resonated with me. I have served as an elder at various churches for the better part of two decades' time, and so I've nearly memorized those biblical instructions along the way, serving as something of a roadmap for navigating the role. They show up in Titus 1 and 1 Timothy 3 and instruct an elder, for instance, to be "faithful to his wife, a man whose children...are not open to the charge of being wild,"[27] to be one who manages "his own family well" and sees to it that "his children obey him."[28] These passages are chock full with "his" and "him" and "man."

Moreover, at the close of the 1 Timothy passage in question, verse 11 then gives explicit instruction to women: "In the same way, the women are to be worthy of respect, not malicious talkers but temperate and trustworthy in everything," which seems to add insult to injury for egalitarians in our midst. If Paul, under the inspiration of the Holy Spirit, intended to include women in the role of elders and/or deacons, wouldn't he have done so here? Instead, he laid out clear instructions for male leaders of the church and then laid out clear instructions for women—who, presumably, would not be serving in these roles.

On the surface, this is a clear case of the apostle Paul using literal language, and he literally excludes women from the church's senior-most leadership roles.

And yet.

The same apostle who quite literally excluded women from serving as an elder or a deacon in one passage draws attention to a woman named Phoebe in another passage, a woman he declares as a "deacon" worthy of respect, a female senior-most church leader Paul praises to every ear listening, for being a key supporter of kingdom work.[29]

So, which is it? What gives, Paul?

Can women be elders, or can't they? Can they be deacons, or can't they? Can they be ordained, *bona fide* leaders, or can't they? Which position, in the end, is "right"?

One of the best books I've ever read on this

subject is *Daughters of the Church* by Ruth A. Tucker and Walter Liefeld. In the authors' thoughtful closing statements, which follow an exhaustive, five-hundred-plus-page dissection of the issue, they write, "Therefore it would appear that while arguments concerning women's ordination (whether pro or con) may be meaningful with regard to denominational polity, there is no passage within the New Testament dealing with ordination to clerical office as usually conceived today on which such arguments can be based."[30]

Do you see? *Nobody's* argument is bulletproof here. But perhaps that's not such a bad thing.

N. T. Wright is a brilliant writer, an Anglican bishop, a New Testament scholar, a Research Professor of New Testament and Early Christianity at St. Andrews University in Scotland, and also a former head of the Church of England for nearly a decade's time. This is a guy who knows his stuff.

Equally true, he knows what he doesn't know.

This is why I like this guy.

On the subject of the ambiguity surrounding anyone's theology, he writes, "The point of discourse is to learn with and from one another. I used to tell my students that at least 20 percent of what I was telling them was wrong, but I didn't know which 20 percent it was: I make many mistakes in life, in relationships and in work, and I don't expect to be free of them in my thinking. But whereas in much of life one's mistakes are often fairly obvious—the shortcut path that ended in a bed of nettles, the experimental recipe that gave us all queasy stomachs, the golf shot that landed in the lake—in the life of the mind things are often not so straightforward."[31]

The reason I appreciate Wright's candor here is that in my experience, those who suppose they have figured out all there is to figure out about God rarely are extravagant worshipers. We don't chase what we've already caught. We don't seek out what we've already secured.

Certainly, there are things we "know that we know" about God—creeds, for example, bedrock issues of faith that simply aren't up for debate. But aren't there thousands more things that we still wonder about, things we take strong positions on but in our heart of hearts say, "You know, I really don't know"?

Here's an image that is helpful to me, a kind of visual goal I keep close by: I want to keep my feet planted on the solid rock of truth, while my head stays in the swirling clouds of mystery—those things I just don't know about God.

Whether we're talking about the silencing of women or the ordination of women or whether you can root against the LSU Tigers and still call yourself a Christian, I want to stay open, curious, eager to be swept away by the wonder that is God himself. Feet on the rock, head in the clouds. This is a very good way to live.

###

Notes

1. Eugene Peterson, *The Pastor: A Memoir,* (New York: HarperCollins Publishers, 2011), 28.

2. Ibid.

3. John MacArthur, *Divine Design: God's Complementary Roles for Men and Women,* (Colorado Springs, CO: David C. Cook, 2011), 138.

4. Alan F. Johnson, Gen. Ed., *How I Changed My Mind About Women in Leadership: Compelling Stories from Prominent Evangelicals,* (Grand Rapids, MI: Zondervan, 2010), 108.

5. NIV, emphasis added, (all four verses).

6. Carolyn Custis James, *Half the Church: Recapturing God's Global Vision for Women,* (Grand Rapids, MI: Zondervan, 2011), 115.

7. http://www.ted.com/talks/sheryl_sandberg_why_we_have_too_few_women_leaders.html; retrieved 1 April 2013.

8. Charles Trombley, *Who Said Women Can't Teach?,* (South Plainfield, NJ: Bridge Publishing, Inc., 1985), 75.

9. Johnson, 180.

10. Trombley, 143, emphasis mine.

11. Trombley, 157.

12. Genesis 3:10, NIV.

13. In case you haven't read the book either, check out Bill and Pam Farrell's *Men are Like Waffles, Women are Like Spaghetti: Understanding and Delighting in*

Your Differences, (LifeWay Christian Resources, 2007).

14. http://www.economist.com/node/7245949, retrieved 11 March 2013.

15. Peggy Orenstein, *Cinderella Ate My Daughter: Dispatches from the Front Lines of the New Girly-Girl Culture,* (New York: HarperCollins Publishers, 2011), 146.

16. **http://originaljewish.com/posts/35**; retrieved 11 March 2013.

17. James, 75.

18. For a fantastic treatment of this topic, read pages 27-28 of Ruth A. Tucker and Walter Liefeld's book, *Daughters of the Church: Women and Ministry from New Testament Times to the Present,* (Zondervan, 1987).

19. Trombley, 187.

20. For more on this subject, see Trombley's work, *Who Said Women Can't Teach?,* page 92.

21. Acts 2:15-16, author's abridgment.

22. http://www.unifem.org/gender_issues/women_poverty_economics/; retrieved 7 March 2013.

23. Romans 12:6-8, author's abridgment.

24. Adapted from Sarah Mae and Sally Clarkson, *Desperate: Hope for the Mom Who Needs to Breathe,* (Nashville, TN: Thomas Nelson, 2013), 136.

25. I heard Pastor T. D. Jakes use this phrasing at his talk during Gateway Church's "Pink" Conference in 2011.

26. Mae and Clarkson, 118.

27. Titus 1:5.

28. 1 Timothy 3:2,4.

29. See Romans 16:1-2.

30. Ruth A. Tucker and Walter Liefeld, *Daughters of the Church: Women and Ministry from New Testament Times to the Present,* (Grand Rapids, MI: Zondervan, 1987), 471.

31. N. T. Wright, *Justification: God's Plan and Paul's Vision,* (Downers Grove, IL: InterVarsity Press, 2009), 20-21.

About the Author

Brady Boyd is the senior pastor of New Life Church in Colorado Springs. He is married to his college sweetheart, Pam, and together they are the parents of a son named Abram and a daughter named Callie. Let Her Lead is his third book. His other books include Fear No Evil and Sons and Daughters. Follow him on Twitter at @PastorBrady or find out more information about his congregation at www.New-LifeChurch.org.

About Bondfire Books

Bondfire Books is an independent epublisher based in Colorado and New York City. We publish fiction and nonfiction—both originals and backlist titles—by today's top writing talent, from established voices to up-and-comers. Learn more about Bondfire and our complete list of titles at www.bondfirebooks. com. Follow us on Twitter @bondfirebooks and find us on Facebook at facebook.com/bondfirebooks.

Made in the USA
San Bernardino, CA
26 July 2016